Kaleidoscope of Thoughts

Daniela Ciubotariu

Presentation by *BookLeaf Publishing*

Web: www.bookleafpub.com

E-mail: info@bookleafpub.com

ISBN: 9789357691703

First edition 2022

DEDICATION

To Eva and Mircea, with love!

The Power of Beauty

The world seems waiting to be seen
It looked vulnerable; it shivers in silence
It touched me with the dew
Then it touched me with a gentle ray of light,
Imploring me to feel it!
It lets me see its nakedness,
Colors after colors it threw into my soul,
And I've absorbed them
With the astonishment and the madness of a
painter.
I didn't allow myself to cry -
My retina was just capturing the eternity.
Glimpses of my life become a script
My thoughts turn into pictures,
Whereas the Irises live the joy to be alive.
So much color!
The picture is overflowing with today.
What if I'm unable to paint your soul with my
feeling
I will suffocate myself in the conquered beauty.
Watching the Glycine, my heart asked my words
To keep silence!

Autumn feelings

It's Fall. Recalling moments of a lifetime.
A pale sun smiles peacefully
The color of copper conquers the souls
Of those who can see;
Tranquility and peace descend.
The leaves break under selfish steps
The flowers smell spicy,
So earthy;
October seems agitated
With people on the sidewalks!
Autumn - I live life
A tired eye from witnessing so much
I gather into my own safe space.
Silent, in reality I try to compose myself, again.
Do I live, really live this fall?!
Or do I only see it knowing that it exists?
I gaze at the sky kneeling in my heart
for the divine presence,
Drinking wine made with grapes from home
I listen to the forest quietly whispering
A secret and autumnal tale!

About us

I often meditate about Love,
But, however much I write
Or I reflect about it,
It's not enough the life I have,
To just express its endless meaning!
It is so much,
So intense,
Inexhaustible for just one word –
This feeling!
We melt down in moods of love,
Powerless and full of fear
Hurting each other.
Overwhelming is this gift of love to us,
When mind is too opaque to get
What is this mystery of a Soul.
When we are using the cold word
We cut the meaning of this feeling,
Corrupting it in our heart,
In other thousand meanings!
We are crying out through life,
Without understanding,
Why does Love hurt so much!
I get chills in my solitude,
Feeling that each of us,
Cries out the limit of truly feeling Love,

Slaves of theories and definitions,
In a world where God,
We heard,
Gave His Life in loving us!

Becoming

Deep inside me
There is a thirst
A wisdom
From the beginning of the World;
I feel it sometimes...
Deep inside me
There is a voice
A true one
So alive
Unbearable to parts of me
Hurting and healing
Pouring new knowledge
Tracing the path
Out of the cave,
Unchained of fear
Burning without mercy
Making you scream
Beyond voice
Beyond tears
Who am I?
Who am I?
Teach me to understand!
Something dies
And then silence
I rise

Lighter than ever
Floating with joy,
Becoming!

Cleansing

It rains day and night
The sun sits gently
somewhere behind;
From the sky,
Luminous tears
Gently washing the earth
Of all our wounds.
It's raining
Sprinkles of forgiveness
Droplets of peace
Covering my thirsty creases
Secretly promising
the clarity of tomorrow.

Searching for balance

Catch a breath,
My darling.
Let's slow down a bit
Our speed is overwhelming.
Images and moments descend
Within us
Setting down on top of each other
Out of time.
What is this rush
And where does it take us!
It became our ruler
Just like that!
And where is that moment
Where the whole world
Sat down,
Motionless
In our encounter!

Mirroring

Tab after tab
Pages have been covered
All the words gather
Into a story.
Buds in the Sun
Bursting with life
Are giving the tree
Youth, again!
Experiences of life
Are often intertwined
With tears
Towards becoming.
Love and pain
Define the flow of life
Time stops only
When we learn
The calling of holiness.

Joy

Through the sieve of my heart
Moments are sifted
Year after year.
From your smile I know, though,
That there is no such thing
As time!
Distance between hearts
Is measured in calling
Praying
Longing.
Seeing you again is joy
An eternal Here.

Fallen from Love

He had left to find himself
There was no more content
In their Love.
While he was wondering,
"Who am I, where do I run away!"
Never looking back,
She stared dumbfounded at her emptiness
Seeing all that she is now without him
Not remembering herself
As if there was no other way
Just "together".
Looking back again and again.
She learned like a newborn
New steps
With clear eyes
New understandings.
Her heart hoped here and there
That longing will show her lover
His way back to her.
She read somewhere about love
For you see, on this front,
There have been many injuries
Over time.
She read that
Where there is a will
Everything can have
A new beginning.

God's Image

I never hugged you with my arms,
Although,
My arms also bear Love.
I hugged you only with my eyes,
With my smiles
I collected you inside
Caressing my longing for you.
To me your love is sacrament.
And I feel with my heart
The covered fruit
Light metamorphosing your image
Warm hand melting in my hand.
I barely breath
When God chooses
To meet Him this way!

Hands language

My hand seemed touched by cold
More than yours
Though you carry more years
On your shoulders.
Perhaps, while I am always
Touching the world
My skin aged from too much feeling,
And my hand,
Leaving behind childhood's hands
Soft and fine
Gained this beautiful aura
Like a special gift,
Speaking about a dimension of existence,
Writing in time fine lines
Deep in my skin
A story.
I smile at my thought
Looking at our holding hands -
Mine and yours,
And I imagine myself
Possessing a unique power
To read life stories when touching people
Thinking that I already have
Wise hands.

More life

My mom often tells me
That in my childhood
I was fearless.
I love this memory of me,
An image unfamiliar somehow,
Because I, since I remember,
I fought battles after battles with fear
This emotion that takes thousand faces
Fear freezes deep inside me
Hope, courage, and confidence.
So, when I am afraid
I recall this image
from my mom' stories.
I recall this brave child
That with her faith and love
Can move the mountains,
She can face unknown worlds
And she can defend from "monsters"
Everyone she loves.
To be able to humble fear
Through an amazing innocence!
The Joy of pure to be
When you jump into Life's arms,
Clapping
Rising from your falls

With your triumphant smile
Blooming every time.
When did this feeling of fear
Crept into me?
Probably, at the moment when
I realized,
How much I love this fragile life.

Our story

There is a meadow filled with poppies
Between me and you -
A whole sea of Beauty and drunkenness!
When you come to greet me
Nightingales are chirping.
Light in your smile welcomes me
Villages and cities are spreading out
At our tired feet,
And we are searching for meanings.
When I sigh, all the green
Gathered in me with an echo,
Feelings burn voiceless.
Holding your hand, I ask my longing
To leave me now
For you rested me into your arms.
The blue of your eyes
Spoke about things one cannot see.
Bells were sending away
The stillness of the morning,
Greeting the Sky and Earth with Joy,
Feeling the Creator of this world
In all His splendor,
Blessing us
In our love that we received
As a gift,
From life.

While time was spinning

It's a deep winter in my corner of the world
My days are easily sifted
in white and gray.
Wood fire gives warmth in memory
Mulled wine with quince
Stories for long evenings
They bring us together.

The earth is adorned in white
Lights and starry glass sky
hope was born...
hearts melted
bewitched,
Under the beauty of nature,
Like a glittering cloak,
Giving wings to our minds,
Enriching our journey,
Making stories and snowmen,
Thousands of universes.

I share the joy of being
my story
Time sifts its immortality
Under the warmth of humanity,
Asking life to happen!

Encounters

With every person I meet,
I learn something about life.
You open a new room,
In your being
And as a good host,
You are greeting with your light
Or with your shadows
Another soul.
Just take a deep breath
And you can then look in amazement:
"What a huge universe!" -
you might say to yourself.
And between the words
In words, or beyond them,
Beyond what we seem to be
Do you feel the connection or not!
You learn about limits,
You get joy, fullness,
Disappointment or repulsion.
But you know that the other,
Just like you,
He's looking for his way
as best he can
Trying to find out who he is,
Being.

Everyone's Beauty Counts

It often happens that you accompany
With different souls on the way,
You get to appreciate and know them,
They end up loving you too,
And suddenly, you don't know when,
You grow apart
You make an expectation with your mind,
You find reasons to be sad,
And a lot of mistakes,
Of weaknesses and inabilities
To the one who once
Was so dear to you.
And you don't like him anymore,
You don't want him anymore,
Break the invisible link!
You're wondering how that's possible,
In such a big universe,
To see and set on other's falls,
On equally same great limits,
To feed, not the beauty experienced,
But the ugliness who brought us to our knees!
You allow yourself to forget,
of our longing
To complete us in this moment!
When each of us are,
Love from Boundless Love!

Invisible links

The moon had descended behind the hills,
Men had become melancholic
Around the fire
They had gathered
As for millennia.
Amnesiacs somehow
And never more whole!
The stories begin at this point,
And the soul seems to put
The shoes for a new journey,
In the rhythm of imagination,
Or an old legend,
Half true maybe
Hyperbolizing the facts,
Tasting the greatness,
In the form of the word,
As we like it.
The gaze was far away,
The phrases carried made-up images,
I marvel once again,
At this strange union,
Of immortality with death!

In The Realm of Feeling

Away from you,
It hurts.
Like the music of the ocean,
Caught between shores,
Hissing its loneliness
Or maybe the overflow.
Away from you,
Rend.
Like a garden after a storm,
Ruined flowers, stripped trees,
Bareness, like a battered painting,
In the scent of freshness and life.
Away from you,
Agony.
It's the lover's waiting,
With her hypnotized gaze,
The knot that breaks voices,
Shaking knees
In the joy of the heart,
the kiss,
dreaming,
Touching hands, beautiful hands.
Away from you,
Acceptance.
Like peace laid,

In the understanding of nature,
That there is no distance,
In the realm of feeling
just burning
longing
And love... especially love,
Hear me, hear me, please, hear me!

Theories of Being

They say we're connected
Between us,
But also, with everything that is life,
That we are like the cells in our body,
Throbbing in an orderly rhythm,
Extinguishing ourselves ... as orderly,
Each with its purpose and meaning,
For proper operation,
Of Existence.
Thus, we would feed the Universe,
Being a part of it,
And the Universe pulsates in us.
Bodies return to the ground,
And where should the souls go!?
It is said, 'all is here',
Always here,
Always!
Living again and again
Discovering the greatness of being.
Give the earth life,
And the breath touches,
What a wonder
And how many limits in the understanding of
the cell
that wants consciousness.

Meditation on Life

When we die here
Are we born somewhere else!
When voices sigh,
"She is gone!" -
Do they give birth to other voices,
That "She has arrived!"?
For what is our life,
And what is death to us!
A body that comes empty but full of life.
A body then that is abandoned!
So, who can tell,
What is this miracle,
A hidden traveler,
Blinded by a blink of time?
Where do we come from,
How do we sow life,
And where does it go so simple,
Without leaving a clear answer!

Home

You are at home where you feel loved
home is a warm hug,
It's the look that contains you,
A welcoming smile.

Home is when the heart rejoices,
When the soul leaps and sings.
It's a tear made of longing,
From a perfect story
Of you and me.

Home is simplicity,
Reunion and Continuity,
You're at home when peace descends,
You are at home wherever you take with you,
The joy of being alive.
You are home when you love and see
The others belonging
Same as you do.